HAWAIIAN

Sea Life Origami

A BEGINNER'S STEP-BY-STEP GUIDE

WRITTEN BY
Laurie Ide

DESIGNS BY
Karley Ide

MUTUAL PUBLISHING

Library of Congress Cataloging-in-Publication Data

Ide, Laurie Shimizu.
  Easy origami : Hawaiian sea life : a step-by-step guide / written by Laurie Ide ; designs by Karley Ide.
      p. cm.
   ISBN 1-56647-923-1 (softcover : alk. paper)
  1. Origami. 2. Marine animals in art. I. Title.
   TT870.I32 2010
   736'.982--dc22

                              2010021845

ISBN-10: 1-56647-923-1
ISBN-13: 978-1-56647-923-3

Design by Courtney Young

First Printing, August 2010

Mutual Publishing, LLC
1215 Center Street, Suite 210
Honolulu, Hawai'i 96816
Ph: 808-732-1709 / Fax: 808-734-4094
email: info@mutualpublishing.com
www.mutualpublishing.com

Printed in China

Table of Contents

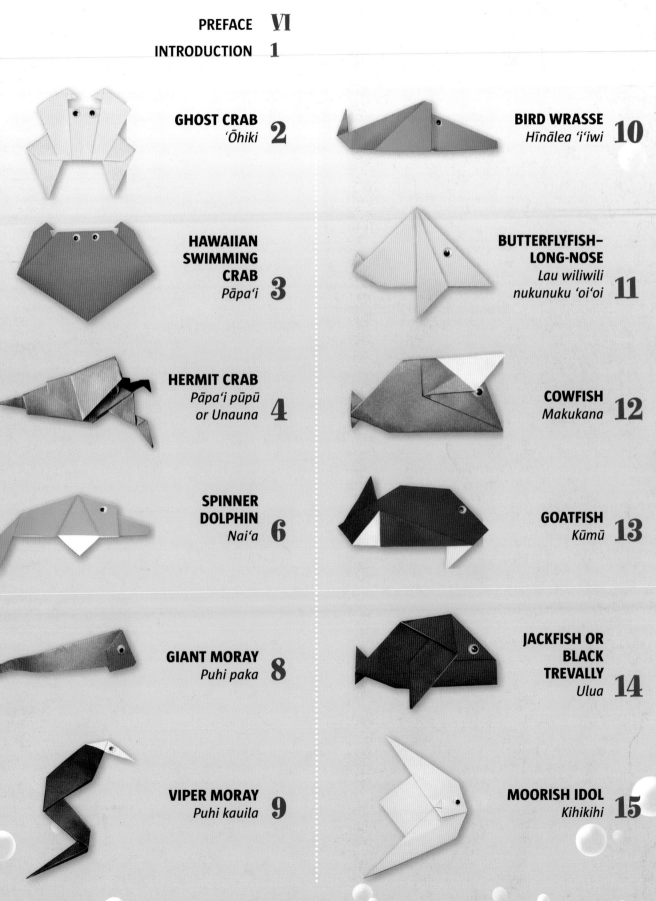

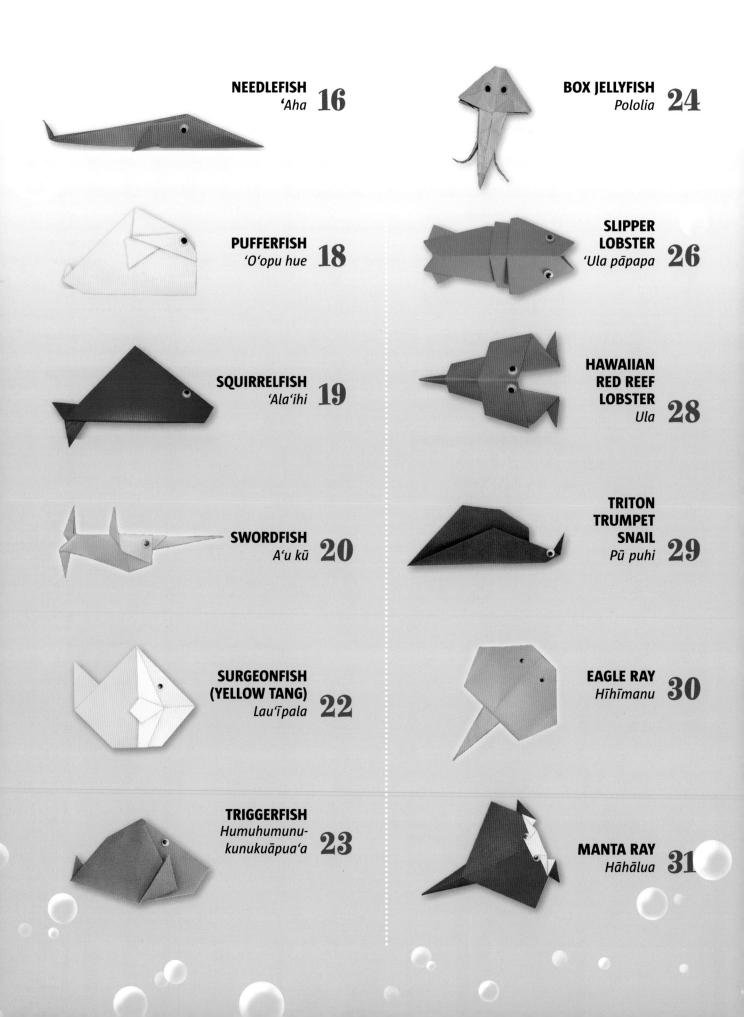

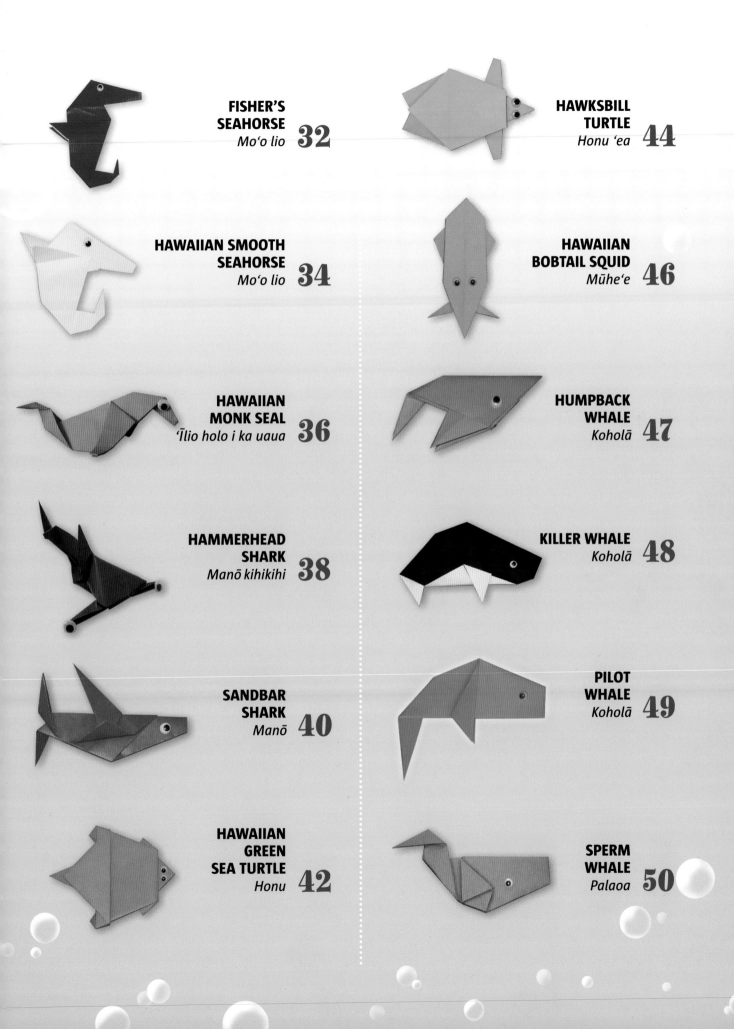

Preface

The designs in this book came about because for the last two years, my daughter, Karley, made origami dinosaurs. She made many different types of dinosaurs. I found them all over the house. I kept throwing them away or placing them in a box.

This past summer vacation, Karley, then ten years old, showed me about twelve to fifteen different sea animal origami models that she made. They were placed on the table. I was shocked. I asked if they were all her creations and not copied from somewhere else. She said they were all her creations. She did not copy them. I checked the internet for images and directions—they were all different.

I ordered books that already existed—they were all different.

This book became a family project. Karley designed the models. Her brother, Kamren, helped with the artwork of cutting and painting. Karl, my husband, helped with the computer advice. I did the folding of the models and the written directions. Auntie Elaine Mezurashi did the editing. The greatest help came from Grandma Shimizu, the photographer. Most of all, we want to thank Mutual Publishing for all their help in publishing this book.

So, here we are now. We want to share these unique designs with you. This book is done in a craft book style. Learn to make different types of crabs, fishes, seahorses, turtles, whales, and many other sea animals. We hope you enjoy it. Our goal is to bring joy and smiles.

Introduction

Origami is the Japanese art of folding paper. *Ori* means "to fold," *gami* means "paper." Origami is very popular in Hawaiʻi. It is also a popular hobby for many people worldwide. Paper folding is found to bring out creative and imaginative skills, develop coordination and logic, stimulate the mind, strengthen the spirit, and exercise the hands. It is great for mental development in children.

Use ordinary printing paper, recycled paper, or origami paper. You can cut a rectangular sheet of paper into a square by folding the top corner down and cutting off the extra piece with scissors. Use a paper cutter for cutting exact squares. Perfectly cut squares make folding easier and neater.

Your local print shops have colored 8½" x 11" paper that is great for origami beginners. For a fee, they will cut it into a square for you. You may buy just a few pieces of paper up to the entire ream. From one ream (five hundred sheets) of paper, you can get five hundred 8½" squares or one thousand 5½" squares. Use twenty- or twenty-four-pound paper. The 8½" squares are perfect for children. It is easier to learn the steps when the paper is large.

You can cut a square out of any recycled paper bag. Use wrapping papers, shopping bags, magazines, and even tea bags. Almost any type of paper can be used as long as it will hold a crease and not tear while being folded. The best paper for folding is fairly thin, un-coated, with a crisp surface. Original origami paper can be purchased at your local craft supply store or on the Internet. They are ready-cut squares in assorted colors. They are usually white in the back. They come in the following standard sizes:

How to cut your own origami squares from 8½" x 11" paper:

8½"

11"

2" x 2"	(5 x 5 cm)
2⅜" x 2⅜"	(6 x 6 cm)
2¾" x 2¾"	(7 x 7 cm)
3" x 3"	(7½ x 7½ cm)
3⅛" x 3⅛"	(8 x 8 cm)
3½" x 3½"	(9 x 9 cm)
3⅞" x 3⅞"	(10 x 10 cm)
4¼" x 4¼"	(11 x 11 cm)
4⅝" x 4⅝"	(12 x 12 cm)
5⅛" x 5⅛"	(13 x 13 cm)
5½" x 5½"	(14 x 14 cm)
5⅞" x 5⅞"	(15 x 15 cm)

Any day, any time, and any place—joy and smiles can be created with origami. Designs like animals, flowers, and almost anything can be created from a piece of paper.

This book shows colored step-by-step photographs and written directions, making it easy to follow. You will see the actual colored photographs. The simple designs in this book can be made in just a few minutes. Once you get familiar with the basic folds, you can begin to create your own designs. New designs are constantly being created. Creating becomes endless!

NOTE: All of the designs in this book were created using a single 5⅞" x 5⅞" sheet of origami paper.

Ghost Crab

'Ōhiki

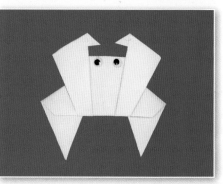

1. Fold the paper in half diagonally.

2. Fold the paper in half diagonally again. Fold from top to bottom left corner.

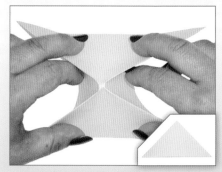

3. Open all folds. Push in the sides of the paper at the crease, forming a point. Press to crease.

4. Fold the bottom sides of the top layer up at an angle.

5. Flip and turn the model. Fold the sides of the top layer inward.

6. Flip and turn the model. Fold the left points inward.

7. Turn the model. Fold the bottom tip up. Tuck the fold under the bottom flaps.

8. Add eyes if desired.

2

Hawaiian Swimming Crab

Pāpaʻi

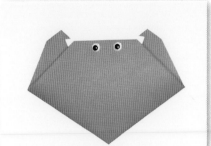

1. Fold the paper in half diagonally.

2. Fold the right tip of the paper upward at an angle.

3. Fold the left tip of the paper upward at an angle.

4. Turn the model. Fold the side tips inward.

5. Turn the model. Fold the bottom point up.

6. Add eyes if desired.

3

Hermit Crab

Pāpaʻi pūpū or Unauna

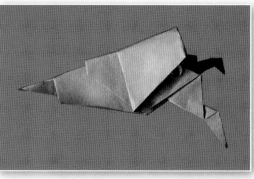

1. Fold the paper in half diagonally.

2. Fold the paper in half diagonally again. Fold from right to left corner.

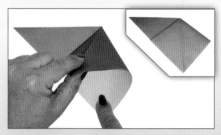

3. Open the triangle pocket on the top. Hold the bottom crease. Pull the left point to the center. Line up the edges, creating a square. Flatten to crease.

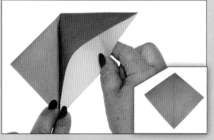

4. Flip the model. Hold the bottom crease. Pull the right point to the center. Line up the edges, creating a square. Flatten to crease.

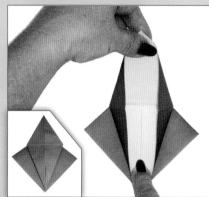

5. Lift up the top layer of the model. Fold the sides inward to the center crease. Line up the edges of the folds, creating a diamond shape. Flatten to crease.

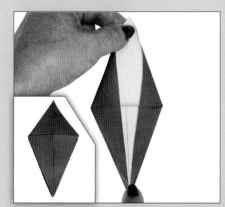

6. Flip the model. Repeat step #5 by lifting up the top layer of the model. Fold the sides inward to the center crease. Line up the edges of the folds, creating a diamond shape. Flatten to crease.

7. Turn the model upside down. Bend the top points outward. Pinch to crease.

8. Bend the side points up. Pinch to crease.

9. Bend the top points outward. Pinch to crease.

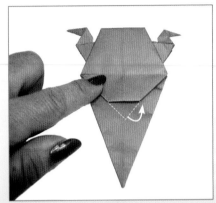

10. Fold up the top layer of the bottom point.

11. Lift the top layer of the bottom of the model up.

12. Fold the bottom tip of the top layer backward.

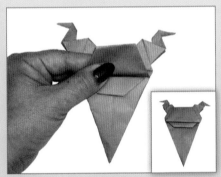

13. Fold the top down and then back up, creating a ¼" pleat.

14. Flip the model. Fold the bottom point up.

15. Fold the bottom point down, creating a ¼" pleat.

16. Fold the model in half.

17. Add eyes if desired.

Spinner Dolphin
Nai'a

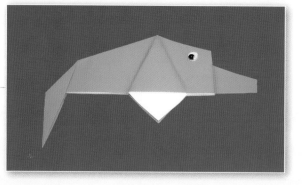

1. Fold the paper in half diagonally.

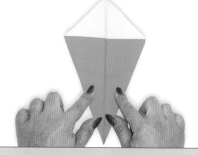

2. Open the fold. Fold the bottom edges inward to the center crease.

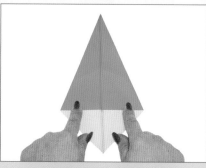

3. Open the folds. Fold the top edges inward to the center crease.

4. Turn the paper. Open the bottom fold. Fold the bottom edges of the paper inward to the center crease, lining up the edges. Pinch the center of the paper up, creating a squared flap. Press the flap down toward the right.

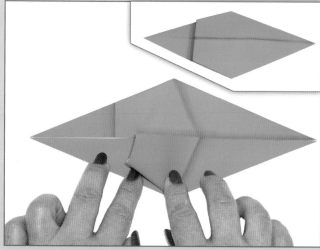

5. Turn the paper. Repeat step #4 for the other side of the model by opening the bottom fold. Fold the bottom edges of the paper up to the center crease, lining up the edges. Pinch the center of the paper, creating a squared flap. Press the flap down toward the left.

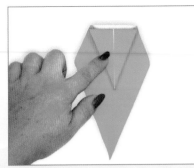  

6. Flip and turn the model, positioning the flaps upward in the back. Fold the top down slightly below the white edge of the flaps.

7. Fold the triangle point up, creating a ¼" pleat.

8. Fold the model in half, positioning the flaps on the outside.

 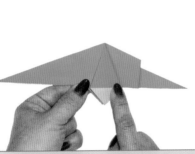 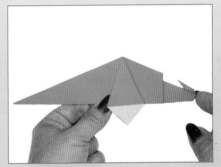

9. Bend the flap backward toward the right.

10. Flip the model. Repeat step #9 by bending the other flap backward toward the left.

11. Fold in the right point by opening the tip and pushing it inward. Pinch to crease.

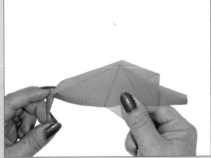 

12. Open the center of the model. Bend the left point down. Pinch to crease.

13. Add eyes if desired.

Giant Moray

Puhi paka

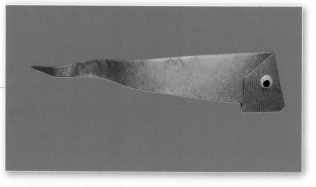

1. Fold the paper in half diagonally.

2. Open the fold. Fold the bottom edges inward to the center crease.

3. Fold the sides inward to the center crease.

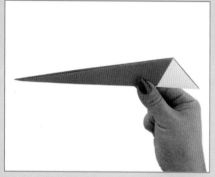

4. Fold the model in half.

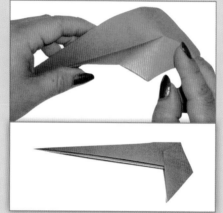

5. Open the last fold. Flip the model. Bend the right tip of the paper down while closing the center fold. Press to crease.

6. Tuck the tip into the center opening of the model. Press to crease.

7. Curl the model using your fingers.

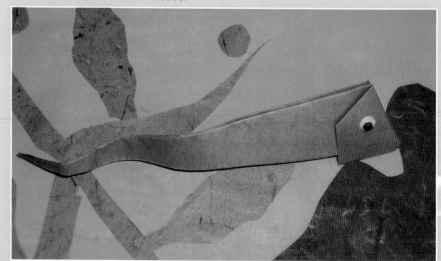

8. Add eyes if desired.

Viper Moray
Puhi kauila

1. Fold the paper in half diagonally.

2. Open the fold. Fold the bottom edges inward to the center crease.

3. Fold the sides inward to the center crease.

4. Fold the model in half.

5. Fold the top-right layer down to the crease.

6. Flip the model. Fold the top-left layer down to the crease.

7. Turn the model. Open the center of the model. Push the top point of the paper down. Close the model. Pinch to crease.

8. Open the center of the model. Push the bottom up. Close the model. Pinch to crease.

9. Open the center of the model. Push the bottom down. Close the model. Pinch to crease.

10. Add eyes if desired.

Bird Wrasse

Hīnālea ʻiʻiwi

1. Fold the paper in half diagonally.

2. Open the fold. Fold the bottom edges inward to the center crease.

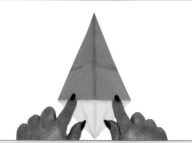

3. Open the folds. Fold the top edges inward to the center crease.

4. Turn the paper. Open the bottom fold. Fold the bottom edges of the paper up to the center crease. Line up the edges, creating a point in the center. Pinch and press down the center point toward the right, lining up the edges.

5. Turn the model. Repeat step #4 by opening the bottom fold. Fold the bottom edges of the paper up to the center crease. Line up the edges, creating a point in the center. Pinch and press down the center point toward the left.

6. Flip the model. Position the triangle flap facing downward in the back. Fold the top down, stopping ¼" from the edge.

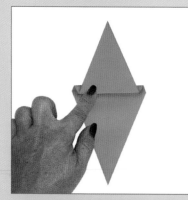

7. Fold the top triangle back up, creating a ¼" pleat.

8. Turn the model. Fold the model in half.

9. Open the top of the model. Push the right point up. Pinch to crease.

10. Flip the model. Open the top of the model. Push the right tip in. Pinch to crease.

11. Add eyes if desired.

Butterflyfish-Long-nose

Lau wiliwili nukunuku ʻoiʻoi

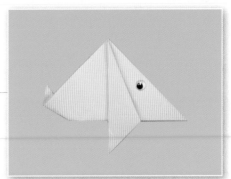

1. Fold the paper in half diagonally.

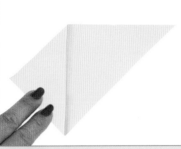

2. Fold the left side of the paper down to the bottom point.

3. Fold the right side of the paper down to the bottom point.

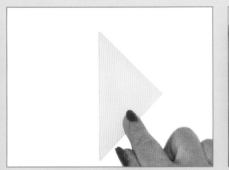

4. Fold the model in half, backward.

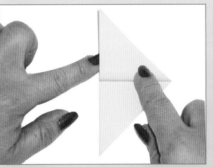

5. Fold the bottom of the top layer of the model up to the top point.

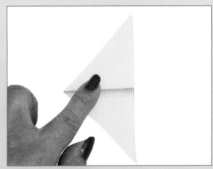

6. Flip the model. Repeat step #5 by folding the bottom of the top layer of the model up to the top point.

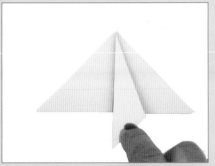

7. Turn the model. Fold the right side of the model inward to the crease.

8. Flip the model. Repeat step #7 by folding the left side of the model inward to the crease.

9. Push the right point up. Pinch to crease.

10. Add eyes if desired.

Cowfish
Makukana

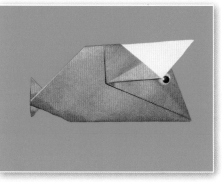

1. Fold the paper in half diagonally.

2. Fold the paper in half diagonally again. Fold from top to bottom right corner.

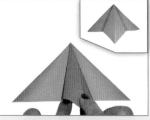

3. Place your left pointer on the bottom center of the model. Pull the right tip just past the center of the paper. Press down to crease.

4. Flip the model. Repeat step #3 by placing your right pointer on the bottom center of the model. Pull the left tip just past the center of the paper. Line up the bottom edges. Press down to crease.

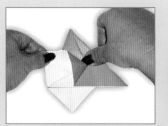

5. Place your left thumb in the opening of the last fold. Place your right thumb fingernail ⅓ of the way from the bottom of the diamond shape. Turn your left thumb upward to form a triangle on the top of your right thumbnail. Line up the left corner. Press down to crease.

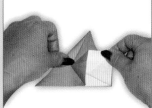

6. Flip the model. Repeat step #5 by placing your right thumb in the opening of the diamond shape. Place your left thumbnail ⅓ of the way from the bottom of the diamond shape. Turn your right thumb upward to form a triangle on the top of your left thumbnail. Line up the corners. Press down to crease.

7. Open the center of the model. Fold the top and bottom sides in, lining up the edges to create points.

8. Fold the model in half.

9. Push up the left point of the model. Pinch to crease.

10. Separate the left point by pulling on the bottom tip half way down. Push your right pointer fingernail down on the center crease of the bottom tip, while gently squeezing the bottom crease with your right hand. The fold should look like an upside-down "W." Pinch the tip to crease.

11. Add eyes if desired.

Goatfish

Kūmū

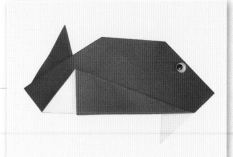

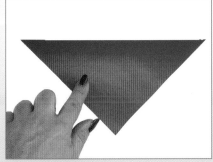

1. Fold the paper in half diagonally.

2. Open the center of the model. Push the right point down. Flatten to crease.

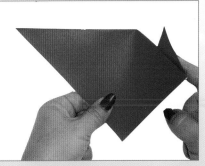

3. Open the top right corner of the model. Push the right point up. Flatten to crease.

4. Fold the bottom of the top layer of the model up to the top fold.

5. Flip the model. Repeat step #4 by folding the bottom up to the top fold.

6. Open the center of the model. Push the right point down until the fold is vertical. Press to crease.

7. Fold the top of the white triangle down to the bottom edge.

8. Flip the model. Repeat step #7 by folding the top of the white triangle down to the bottom edge.

9. Add eyes if desired.

Jackfish or Black Trevally

Ulua

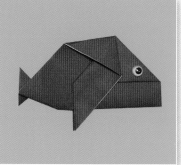

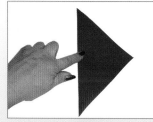

1. Fold the paper in half diagonally.

2. Fold the paper in half diagonally again. Fold from bottom to top corner.

3. Fold the open side of the triangle down slightly past the edge of the paper.

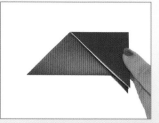

4. Flip the model. Repeat step #3 by folding the top of the triangle down slightly past the edge of the paper.

5. Lift up the top triangle flap. Fold it toward the left, lining up the left edges. Leave ½" uncovered on the bottom.

6. Flip the model. Repeat step #5 by folding the triangle flap toward the right, lining up the right edges. Leave ½" uncovered on the bottom.

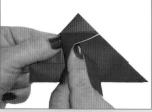

7. Place your right pointer under the top triangle flap. Place your left thumbnail on the left crease of the triangle about ⅓ of the way from the top. Pull down and turn over the flap to the left using your pointer. Press down to crease.

8. Flip the model. Repeat step #7 by placing your left pointer under the top triangle flap. Place your right thumbnail on the right crease of the triangle ⅓ of the way from the top. Pull down and turn over the flap to the right using your pointer. Line up the bottom points. Press down to crease.

9. Open the center of the model. Push up the left point. Pinch to crease.

10. Separate the bottom point.

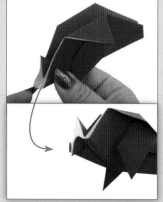

11. Push your left pointer fingernail halfway down on the center crease of the bottom tip, while gently squeezing the bottom crease with your right hand. The fold should look like an upside-down "W." Pinch the tip to crease.

12. Add eyes if desired.

14

Moorish Idol

Kihikihi

1. Fold the paper in half diagonally.

2. Fold the left side of the paper down at an angle leaving about 1" from the edge of the top crease and 1" from the edge of the bottom point.

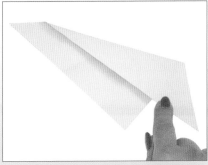

3. Open the last fold. Repeat step #2 for the right side of the model by folding it down at an angle leaving about 1" from the edge of the top crease and 1" from the edge of the bottom point.

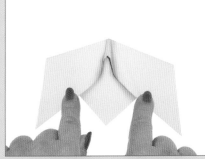

4. Open the last fold. Fold the top points down on the existing creases.

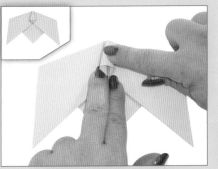

5. Open the center pocket formed in step #4. Use a pointed stick if needed. Press it down, creating a diamond shape.

6. Flip and turn the model. Fold the sides inward, lining up the edges.

7. Add eyes if desired.

Needlefish

'Aha

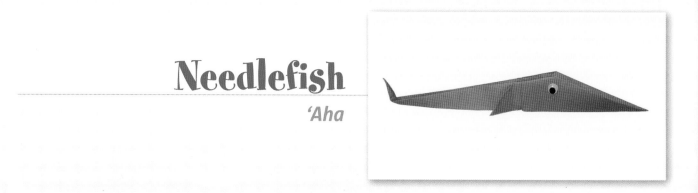

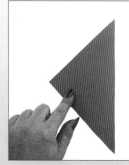

1. Fold the paper in half diagonally.

2. Open the fold. Fold the bottom edges inward to the center crease.

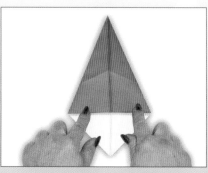

3. Open the folds. Fold the top edges inward to the center crease.

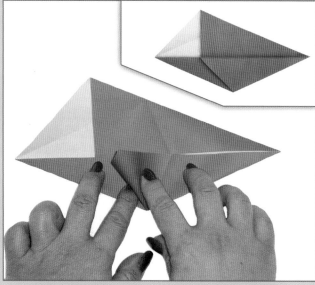

4. Turn the model. Open the bottom fold. Fold the bottom edges of the paper up to the center crease. Line up the edges, creating a point in the center. Pinch and press the point down and toward the left.

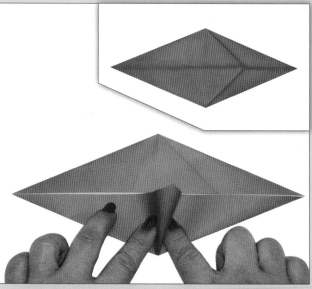

5. Turn the model. Repeat step #4 by opening the bottom fold. Fold the bottom edges of the paper up to the center crease. Line up the edges, creating a point in the center. Pinch and press the point down and toward the right.

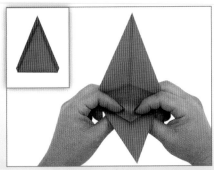

6. Turn the model, positioning the flap downward. Fold the bottom up just below the halfway point.

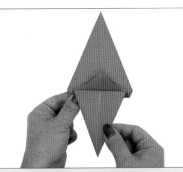

7. Fold the top layer of the triangle down creating a ¼" pleat.

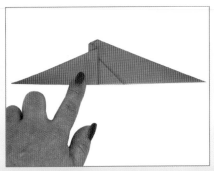

8. Fold the model in half, positioning the flaps on the outside. Turn the model.

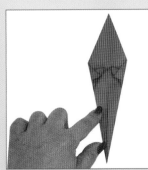

9. Open the last fold. Turn the model. Fold the bottom, longer sides inward to the center crease.

10. Turn the model. Fold the model in half.

11. Open the top of the model. Push the right tip upward. Pinch to crease.

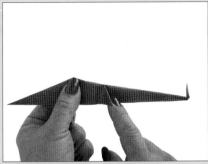

12. Pull out the side flaps on both sides of the model.

13. Add eyes if desired.

Pufferfish

'O'opu hue

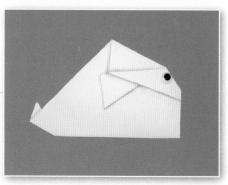

1. Fold the paper in half diagonally.

2. Fold the paper in half diagonally again. Fold from bottom to top corner.

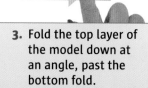

3. Fold the top layer of the model down at an angle, past the bottom fold.

4. Flip the model. Repeat step #3 by folding the top point down at an angle, past the bottom fold.

5. Place your right thumbnail halfway down from the top crease. Place your left pointer inside of the fold. Push and turn over the opening toward your right thumb. Press down to crease.

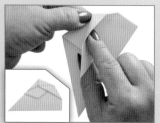

6. Flip the model. Repeat step #5 by placing your left thumbnail halfway down from the top crease. Place your right pointer inside the fold. Push and turn over the opening toward your left thumb. Press down to crease.

7. Fold the tip backward. Tuck it behind the fold to shorten it. Pinch to crease.

8. Flip the model. Repeat step #7 by folding the tip backward. Tuck it behind the fold to shorten it. Pinch to crease.

9. Open the center of the model. Fold the top down ¼". Close the model.

10. Push the right point in. Pinch to crease.

11. Add eyes if desired.

Squirrelfish

'Ala'ihi

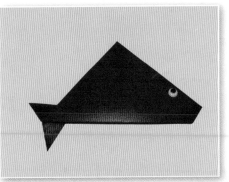

1. Fold the paper in half diagonally.

2. Fold the paper in half diagonally again. Fold from left to right corner.

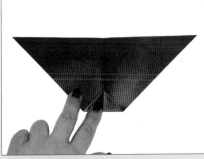

3. Open the last fold. Fold the bottom point upward.

4. Fold the model in half.

5. Turn the model. Fold the bottom edge up ½" at an angle.

6. Fold the top layer of the right point down. Flip the model.

7. Add eyes if desired.

Swordfish

A'u kū

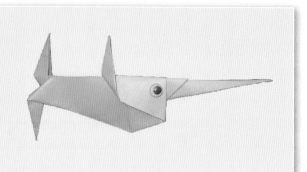

1. Fold the paper in half diagonally.

2. Fold the paper in half diagonally again. Fold from left to right corner.

3. Open the triangle pocket on the top. Hold the bottom. Pull the right point to the center. Line up the edges, creating a square. Flatten to crease.

4. Flip the model. Hold the bottom. Pull the left point to the center. Line up the edges, creating a square. Flatten to crease.

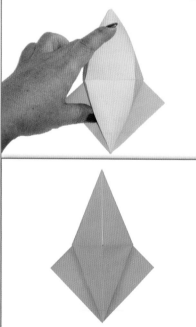

5. Lift up the top layer of the model. Fold the sides inward to the center crease. Line up the edges of the folds, creating a diamond shape. Press to crease.

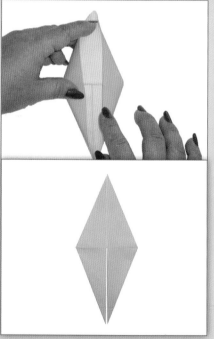

6. Flip the model. Repeat step #5 by lifting up the top layer of the model. Fold the sides inward to the center crease. Line up the edges to the center crease, creating a diamond shape. Press to crease.

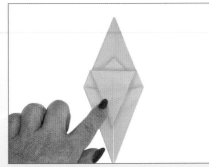

7. Fold the top layer down, just above the center crease.

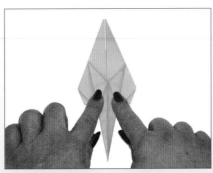

8. Flip and turn the model, positioning the open end on the top. Fold the bottom sides toward the center crease.

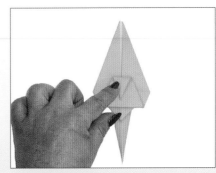

9. Flip the model. Fold the tip of the top layer down about halfway.

10. Fold the model in half. Pinch and pull up the point of the last fold.

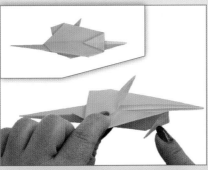

11. Open the center of the model. Open the bottom fold. Fold the point inward ¾". Pinch to crease.

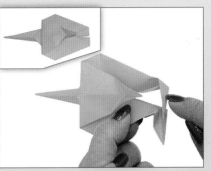

12. Open the top fold. Fold the point downward ¾". Pinch to crease.

13. Fold the model in half.

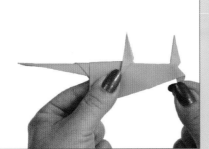

14. Pull out the top and bottom points on the right, making them vertical to each other. Pinch to crease.

15. Add eyes if desired.

Surgeonfish (Yellow Tang)

Lauʻīpala

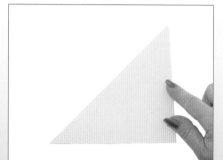

1. Fold the paper in half diagonally.

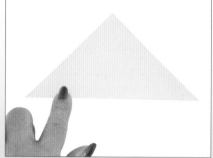

2. Fold the paper in half diagonally again. Fold from top to bottom corner.

3. Open the triangle pocket on the top. Push it to the right matching the bottom edges. Press it down to crease.

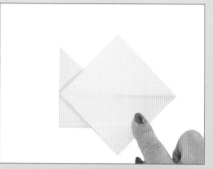

4. Turn the model, positioning the crease horizontally. Fold the bottom triangle halfway up toward the back.

5. Fold the small bottom triangle up against the folded crease.

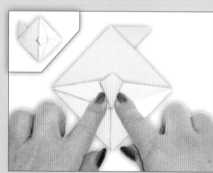

6. Open the last fold. Push in the fold along the existing creases.

7. Turn the model. Fold the top layer of the open side of the model up. Create a center flap in the middle.

8. Create a triangle with the center flap by pushing the sides inward toward the center. Press down to crease.

9. Flip and turn the model. Fold the small triangle up against the crease. Tuck in the triangle between the fold.

10. Add eyes if desired.

Triggerfish

Humuhumunukunukuāpuaʻa

1. Fold the paper in half diagonally.

2. Fold the paper in half diagonally again. Fold from left to right corner.

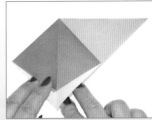

3. Open the triangle pocket on the top. Hold the bottom. Pull the right point toward the center. Line up the edges, creating a square. Flatten to crease.

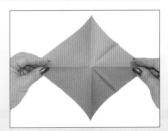

4. Open all folds. Position the creased square to the right. Pinch both sides of the paper.

5. Push in the right side of paper (the side with the creased square), while pinching the top and bottom sides together. Press to crease.

6. Fold the top layer of the bottom-right point upward.

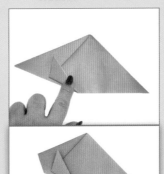

7. Flip the model. Repeat step #6 by folding the bottom-left point upward.

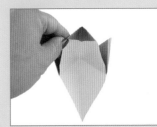

8. Open the center of the model. Fold in the top point of the paper. Close the center of the model.

9. Push in the right point of the model. Press to crease.

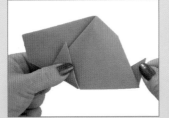

10. Fold the bottom point back up at an angle. Press to crease.

11. Add eyes if desired.

23

Box Jellyfish
Pololia

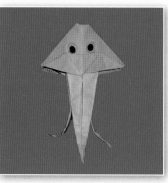

1. Fold the paper in half diagonally.

2. Fold the paper in half diagonally again. Fold from right to left corner.

3. Open the triangle pocket on the top. Hold the bottom crease. Pull the left point toward the center. Line up the edges, creating a square. Flatten to crease.

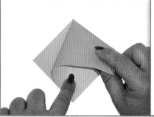 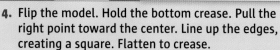

4. Flip the model. Hold the bottom crease. Pull the right point toward the center. Line up the edges, creating a square. Flatten to crease.

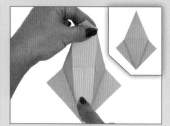

5. Lift up the top layer of the model. Fold the sides inward to the center crease. Line up the edges of the folds, creating a diamond shape. Press to crease.

6. Flip the model. Repeat step #5 by lifting up the top layer of the model. Fold the sides inward to the center crease. Line up the edges, creating a diamond shape. Press to crease.

7. Open the sides by pinching the top and bottom layer of the model together. Turn the model.

8. Fold the bottom points up on the front and back of the model.

9. Fold the top layer down, creating a ¼" pleat.

10. Flip the model. Repeat step #9 by folding the top layer down, creating a ¼" pleat.

24

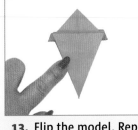

11. Open the sides by pinching the top and bottom layer of the model together.

12. Fold the top layer down, creating a ¼" pleat.

13. Flip the model. Repeat step #12 by folding the top point down, creating a ¼" pleat.

14. Fold the bottom sides of the top layer of the model inward to the center crease. Two triangle pockets will form at the top. Flatten to crease.

15. Flip the model. Repeat step #14 by folding the bottom sides of the model inward to the center crease. Two triangle pockets will form at the top. Flatten to crease.

16. Open the sides by pinching the top and bottom layer of the model together.

17. Fold the bottom sides inward to the center crease. Two triangle pockets will form at the top. Flatten to crease.

18. Flip the model. Repeat step #17 by folding the bottom sides inward to the center crease. Two triangle pockets will form at to the top. Flatten to crease.

19. Pull out the four corners at the top to puff up the center tip. Push in to flatten the top using your fingernail.

20. Curl the four points outward using a pencil.

21. Add eyes if desired.

Slipper Lobster

'Ula pāpapa

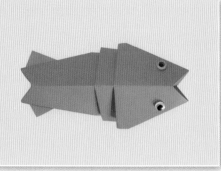

1. Fold the paper in half lengthwise.

2. Fold the paper in half lengthwise again.

3. Open the last fold. Fold the bottom corners inward to the center crease, creating two long triangles.

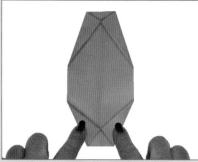

4. Turn the model. Fold the bottom corners inward to the center crease, creating two smaller triangles.

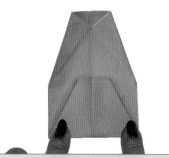

5. Fold the bottom of the model up.

6. Fold the back of the paper down, creating a ⅛" pleat.

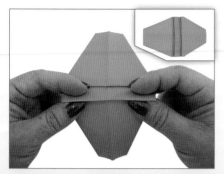

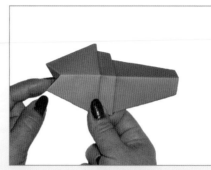

7. Pinch the paper together ½" below the previous crease. Flatten the pinched flap facing downward.

8. Fold the model in half.

9. Push in the left center of the model.

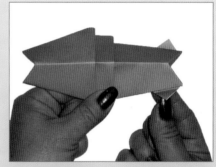

10. Push in the right center of the model.

11. Flip and open the center of the model. Fold the two corners outward.

12. Close the model. Bend the two corners up against the folded edge.

13. Add eyes if desired.

Hawaiian Red Reef Lobster

Ula

1. Fold the paper in half diagonally.

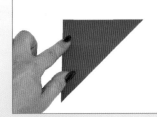

2. Fold the paper in half diagonally again. Fold from left to right corner.

3. Open the last fold. Fold the sides inward to the center crease.

4. Fold the top points outward.

5. Flip the model. Fold the top points inward against the existing fold.

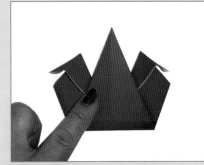

6. Flip the model. Fold the bottom point up.

7. Fold the top point down, creating a ¼" pleat.

8. Fold the bottom point up and then back down, creating a ¼" pleat.

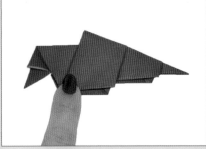

9. Fold the model in half.

10. Add eyes if desired.

Triton Trumpet Snail

Pū puhi

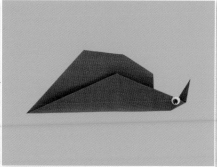

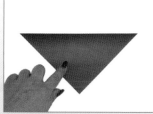

1. Fold the paper in half diagonally.

2. Fold the paper in half diagonally again. Fold from left to right corner.

3. Open the triangle pocket on the top. Hold the bottom crease. Pull the right point toward the center. Line up the edges, creating a square. Flatten to crease.

4. Lift up the top layer of the model. Fold the sides inward to the center crease. Line up the edges, creating a diamond shape. Flatten to crease.

5. Fold the diamond shape in half by bending it backward. Turn the model.

6. Fold the right point upward.

7. Flip the model. Fold the top of the triangle downward, at an angle, to the edge of the paper.

8. Tuck the tip under the fold.

9. Flip the model. Open the center of the model. Push in the top. Pinch to crease.

10. Add eyes if desired.

29

Eagle Ray
Hīhīmanu

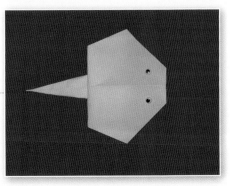

1. Fold the paper in half diagonally.

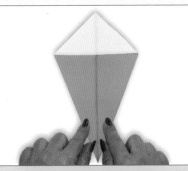

2. Fold the bottom sides inward to the center crease.

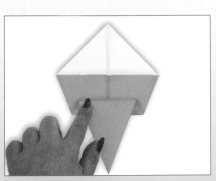

3. Fold the bottom point up, then back down, creating a ⅝" pleat.

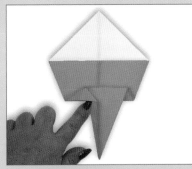

4. Fold the left side of the tail inward to the center crease. Start at the bottom. A triangle pocket will form at to the top of the fold. Flatten to crease.

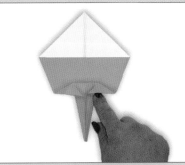

5. Repeat step #4 for the right side of the tail by folding it inward to the center crease. Start at the bottom. A triangle pocket will form at the top of the fold. Flatten to crease.

6. Fold the top point down.

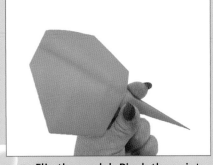

7. Flip the model. Pinch the point to thin it.

8. Curl the sides using a pencil.

9. Add eyes if desired.

Manta Ray

Hāhālua

1. Fold the paper in half diagonally.

2. Fold the paper in half diagonally again. Fold from left to right corner.

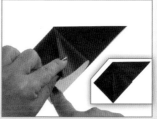

3. Open the triangle pocket on the top. Hold the bottom crease. Pull the right point to the center. Line up the edges, creating a square. Flatten to crease.

4. Flip the model. Hold the bottom crease. Pull the left point to the center. Line up the edges, creating a square. Flatten to crease.

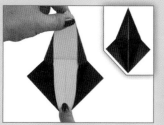

5. Lift up the top layer of the model. Fold the sides inward to the center crease. Line up the edges of the folds, creating a diamond shape. Press to crease.

6. Turn the model. Fold the bottom sides of the model inward to the center crease.

7. Bend the two top center points outward. Press to crease.

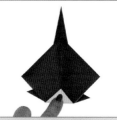

8. Flip and turn the model. Fold the bottom point up. Make a ½" fold.

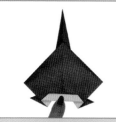

9. Fold the bottom up again.

10. Turn the model. Create a pocket by placing your left pointer on the edge of the folded flap. Place your right pointer under the folded flap. Push the flap toward the left using your right pointer, creating a pocket. Press down to crease.

11. Repeat step #10 by placing your right pointer on the edge of the folded flap. Place your left pointer under the folded flap. Push the flap toward the right using your left pointer, creating a pocket. Press down to crease.

12. Add eyes if desired.

Fisher's Seahorse

Mo'o lio

1. Fold the paper in half diagonally.

2. Open the fold. Fold the bottom edges inward to the center crease.

3. Open the folds. Fold the top edges inward to the center crease.

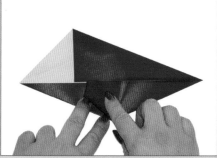

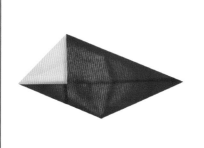

4. Turn the model. Open the bottom fold. Fold the bottom edges of the paper up to the center crease. Line up the edges, creating a squared flap in the center. Pinch and press the flap down toward the left.

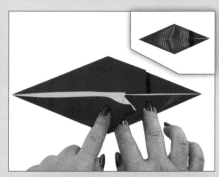

5. Turn the model. Repeat step #4 by opening the bottom fold. Fold the bottom edges of the paper up to the center crease. Line up the edges, creating a squared flap in the center. Pinch and press the flap down toward the right.

6. Flip the model. Face the flaps downward in the back of the model. Fold the top point down, stopping before the bottom edge.

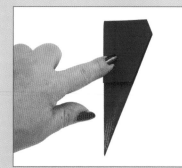

7. Fold the model in half, positioning the flaps on the outside.

8. Pull out the point from inside the folded model. Press to crease.

32

9. Fold the right tip in. Press to crease.

10. Open the center of the model. Fold the bottom point up.

11. Close the center of the model. Pull out the bottom point. Press to crease.

12. Open the center of the model. Fold the bottom tip up.

13. Close the center of the model. Pull out the tip. Press to crease.

14. Fold the front and backside of the flaps upward.

15. Fold each flap in half, downward.

16. Add eyes if desired.

Hawaiian Smooth Seahorse

Mo'o lio

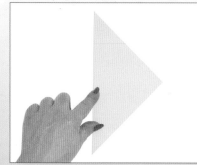

1. Fold the paper in half diagonally.

2. Open the fold. Fold the bottom edges inward to the center crease.

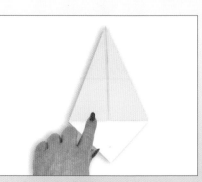

3. Open the folds. Fold the top edges inward to the center crease.

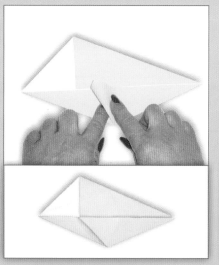

4. Turn the model. Open the bottom fold. Fold the bottom edges of the paper up to the center crease. Line up the edges, creating a point in the center. Pinch and press down the point toward the left.

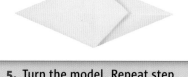

5. Turn the model. Repeat step #4 by opening the bottom fold. Fold the bottom edges of the paper up to the center crease. Line up the edges, creating a point in the center. Pinch and press down the point toward the right.

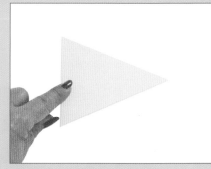

6. Fold the model in half.

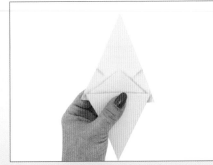

7. Turn the model. Fold the top layer down, creasing just above the fold.

8. Fold the model in half lengthwise, positioning the flaps on the outside.

9. Open the center of the model. Bend down the top point to the right. Pinch to crease.

10. Push in the right tip. Pinch to crease.

11. Open the center of the model. Push up the bottom point toward the right. Pinch to crease.

12. Open the center of the model. Fold the bottom point up.

13. Close the model. Pull out the bottom tip. Pinch to crease.

14. Bend down the front and backside of the flaps.

15. Add eyes if desired.

Hawaiian Monk Seal

ʻĪlio holo i ka uaua

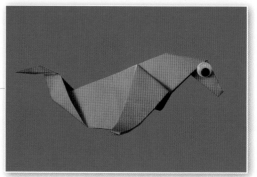

1. Fold the paper in half diagonally.

2. Fold the paper in half diagonally again. Fold from right to left corner.

3. Open the triangle pocket on the top. Hold the bottom. Pull the left point toward the center. Line up the edges, creating a square. Flatten to crease.

4. Flip the model. Hold the bottom crease. Pull the right point to the center. Line up the edges, creating a square. Flatten to crease.

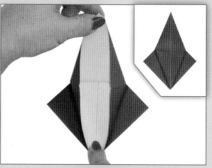

5. Lift up the top layer of the model. Fold the sides inward. Line up the edges to the center crease, creating a diamond shape. Flatten to crease.

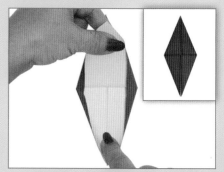

6. Flip the model. Repeat step #5 by lifting up the top layer of the model. Fold the sides inward to the center crease. Line up the edges to the center crease, creating a diamond shape. Flatten to crease.

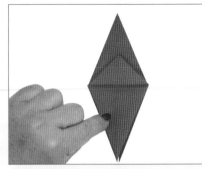

7. Fold the top layer down.

8. Fold the model in half. Fold from left to right.

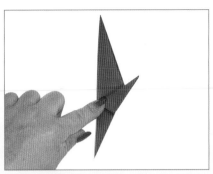

9. Fold the top layer of the bottom point up at an angle, just below the center crease.

10. Flip the model. Repeat step #9 by folding the top layer of the bottom point up at an angle, just below the center crease.

11. Open the center of the model. Open the two side points. Fold each tip inward. Press to crease. Close the center of the model.

12. Flip the model. Open the center fold. Push the right point of the model down. Pinch to crease.

13. Open the center fold. Fold the bottom tip up. Pinch to crease.

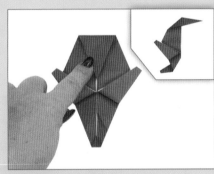

14. Open the center of the model. Fold the top point down. Close the model. Pull out the point. Pinch to crease.

15. Flip the model. Turn the model. Open the center of the model. Bend the left tip backward. Pinch to crease.

16. Curl the flaps on both sides using a pencil.

17. Add eyes if desired.

Hammerhead Shark

Manō kihikihi

1. Fold the paper in half diagonally.

2. Fold the paper in half diagonally again. Fold from right to left corner.

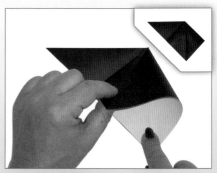

3. Open the triangle pocket on the top. Hold the bottom crease. Pull the left point to the center. Line up the edges, creating a square. Flatten to crease.

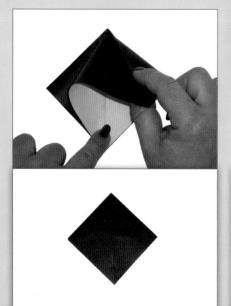

4. Flip the model. Hold the bottom crease. Pull the right point to the center. Line up the edges, creating a square. Flatten to crease.

5. Lift up the top layer of the model. Fold the sides inward. Line up the edges to the center crease, creating a diamond shape. Flatten to crease.

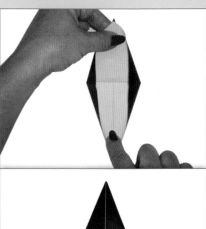

6. Flip the model. Repeat step #5 by lifting up the top layer of the model. Fold the sides inward to the center crease. Line up the edges, creating a diamond shape. Flatten to crease.

7. Fold the top layer of the model down.

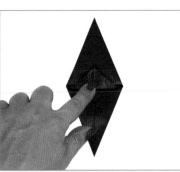

8. Fold the triangle point down, then back up creating a ¼" pleat.

9. Fold the model in half, positioning the flap on the outside. Open the center fold. Push the top point down. Press to crease.

10. Push the top point back up, stopping just before the previous crease. Press to crease.

11. Turn the model. Open the center of the model. Open and push down the top points until they are horizontal to each other. Press to crease.

12. Open and fold in the side points. Press to crease.

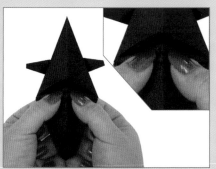

13. Flip the model. Close the model slightly while making a triangle crease with your fingernails.

14. Fold the model in half. Pull out the top point.

15. Open the center of the model. Flip the model. Bend the top down.

16. Flip the model. Make an upward crease on both sides of the model. Use a fingernail file.

17. Close the model. Push the left center of the model inward on the crease.

18. Add eyes if desired. Add tape inside the model, to create a narrow body (optional).

Sandbar Shark

Manō

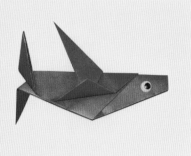

1. Fold the paper in half diagonally.

2. Fold the paper in half diagonally again. Fold from right to left corner.

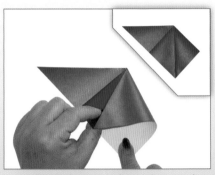

3. Open the triangle pocket on the top. Hold the bottom crease. Pull the left point to the center. Line up the edges, creating a square. Flatten to crease.

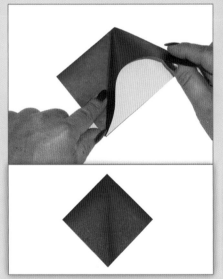

4. Flip the model. Hold the bottom. Pull the right point to the center. Line up the edges, creating a square. Flatten to crease.

5. Lift up the top layer of the model. Fold the sides inward. Line up the edges to the center crease, creating a diamond shape. Flatten to crease.

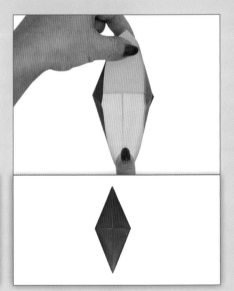

6. Flip the model. Repeat step #5 by lifting up the top layer of the model. Fold the sides inward to the center crease. Line up the edges, creating a diamond shape. Flatten to crease.

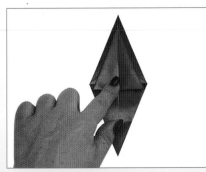

7. Bend down the top layer of the model. Fold it back up ¼" below the center fold.

8. Fold the top triangle layer back down, ½" above the previous crease.

9. Fold the model in half.

10. Turn the model. Pull the right flap out.

11. Fold the top layer of the bottom tip of the model to the right.

12. Fold the bottom tip backward toward the left.

13. Open the center of the model. Fold the top down. Close the model.

14. Turn the model. Make an upward crease on the top layer of both sides of the model. Use a fingernail file (optional).

15. Add eyes if desired.

Hawaiian Green Sea Turtle

Honu

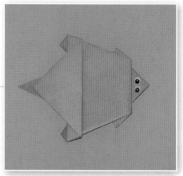

1. Fold the right side of the paper inward 1¼".

2. Fold the bottom side of the paper inward 1¼".

3. Turn the paper. Open both folds. Close both folds back down, running your finger from the bottom to the top to create a hood-shaped point.

4. Flatten the point by pushing it down, creating a square.

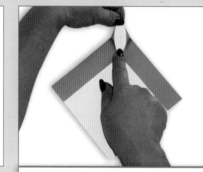

5. Lift up the square flap. Hold the bottom on the center crease. Fold the sides inward toward the center crease. Line up the edges, creating a diamond shape. Flatten to crease.

6. Fold the top down.

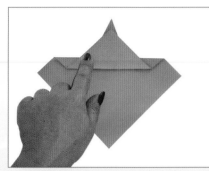

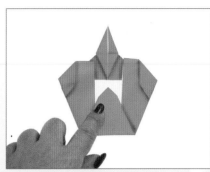

7. Flip the model. Fold the top edge down ½", lifting up the point from the back.

8. Flip the model. Fold the sides inward.

9. Fold the bottom point up.

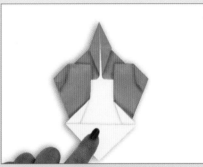

10. Open the last two folds. Pull the bottom corners outward. Fold the bottom point up. Press to crease.

11. Fold the bottom flap down, leaving a ¼" pleat in the back.

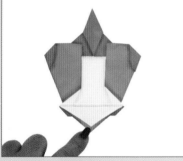

12. Fold the bottom edges in.

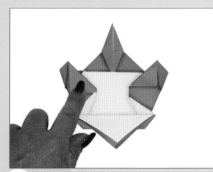

13. Fold the inside corners down.

14. Add eyes if desired.

Hawksbill Turtle

Honu 'ea

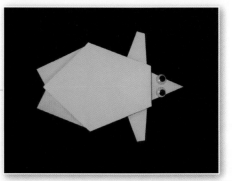

1. Fold the paper in half diagonally.

2. Fold the paper in half diagonally again. Fold from right to left corner.

3. Open the triangle pocket on the top. Hold the bottom crease. Pull the left point to the center. Line up the edges, creating a square. Flatten to crease.

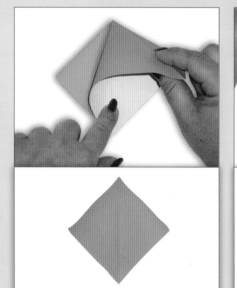

4. Flip the model. Hold the bottom crease. Pull the right point to the center. Line up the edges, creating a square. Flatten to crease.

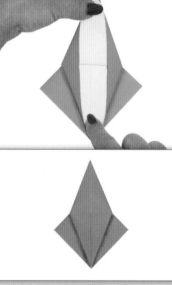

5. Lift up the top layer of the model. Fold the sides inward. Line up the edges, creating a diamond shape. Flatten to crease.

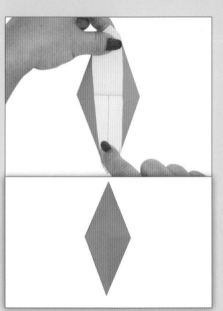

6. Flip the model. Repeat step #5 by lifting up the top layer of the model. Fold the sides inward to the center crease. Line up the edges, creating a diamond shape. Flatten to crease.

7. Fold the top layer of the model down.

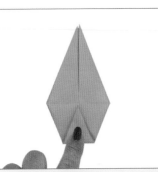

8. Flip and turn the model. Position the open tip on the top. Fold the bottom point up to the center crease.

9. Push the top points outward. Pinch to crease.

10. Open the side points. Fold in the tips. Close the side points. Pinch to crease.

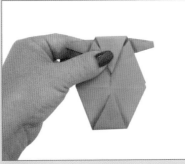

11. Fold the top of the model down.

12. Fold the top of the model back up, creating a ⅛" pleat.

13. Fold the model in half.

14. Push in the right side of the model. Pinch to crease.

15. Add eyes if desired.

Hawaiian Bobtail Squid

Mūheʻe

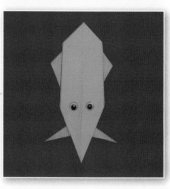

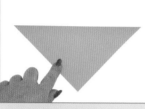

1. Fold the paper in half diagonally.

2. Fold the paper in half diagonally again. Fold from right to left corner.

3. Open the triangle pocket on the top. Hold the bottom crease. Pull the left point to the center. Line up the edges, creating a square. Flatten to crease.

4. Flip the model. Hold the bottom crease. Pull the right point to the center. Line up the edges, creating a square. Flatten to crease.

5. Lift up the top layer of the model. Fold the sides inward to the center crease. Line up the edges, creating a diamond shape. Flatten to crease.

6. Flip the model. Repeat step #5 by lifting up the top layer of the model. Fold the sides inward to the center crease. Line up the edges, creating a diamond shape. Press to crease.

7. Fold the top points down on both the front and backside of the model.

8. Fold the sides inward and then back outward.

9. Flip and turn the model. Bend the two inside thin points outward, parallel to each other. Pinch to crease.

10. Add eyes if desired.

Humpback Whale
Koholā

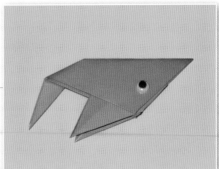

1. Fold the paper in half diagonally.

2. Fold the paper in half diagonally again. Fold from left to right corner.

3. Open the triangle pocket on the top. Hold the bottom crease. Pull the right point to the center. Line up the edges, creating a square. Flatten to crease.

4. Flip the model. Hold the bottom crease. Pull the left point to the center. Line up the edges, creating a square. Flatten to crease.

5. Lift up the top layer of the model. Fold the sides inward. Line up the edges, creating a diamond shape. Flatten to crease.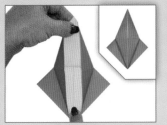

6. Flip the model. Repeat step #5 by lifting up the top layer of the model. Fold the sides inward to the center crease. Line up the edges, creating a diamond shape. Flatten to crease.

7. Turn the model. Fold the right points downward at an angle on both sides of the model.

8. Fold the model in half, positioning the flaps on the inside.

9. Open the center of the model. Fold the side points down against the crease.

10. Tuck in the two folds created in step #9. Pinch to crease.

11. Close the model. Push down the right point. Press to crease.

12. Add eyes if desired.

Killer Whale (Orca)

Koholā

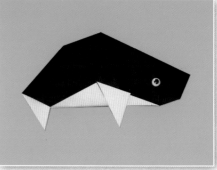

1. Fold the paper in half diagonally.

2. Fold the paper in half diagonally again. Fold from left to right corner.

3. Open the triangle pocket on the top. Hold the bottom. Pull the right point to the center. Line up the edges, creating a square. Flatten to crease.

4. Fold the square in half on the crease, by folding it backward.

5. Hold the inside center points together. Pull out the outside point, lining up the outside crease with the inside center points.

6. Slightly open the center of the model. Fold the top point down. Close the model.

7. Fold the bottom point of the top layer up.

8. Flip the model. Repeat step #7 by folding the bottom point up.

9. Fold the white point down.

10. Flip the model. Repeat step #9 by folding the white point down.

11. Push in the right point. Pinch to crease.

12. Add eyes if desired.

Pilot Whale

Koholā

1. Fold the paper in half diagonally.

2. Open the fold. Fold the bottom edges inward to the center crease.

3. Open the folds. Fold the top edges inward to the center crease.

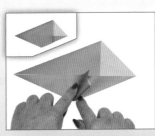

4. Turn the model. Open the bottom fold. Fold the bottom edges of the paper up to the center crease. Line up the edges, creating a squared flap in the center. Pinch and press down the flap toward the right.

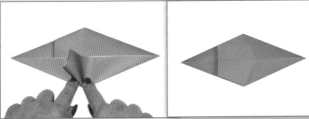

5. Turn the model. Repeat step #4 by opening the bottom fold. Fold the bottom edges of the paper up to the center crease. Line up the edges, creating a squared flap in the center. Pinch and press down the flap toward the left.

6. Flip the model. Place the flaps on the bottom facing the left. Fold the right point inward.

7. Fold the model in half, positioning the flaps on the outside.

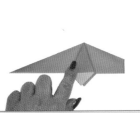

8. Fold the front and back flaps forward.

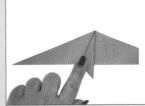

9. Fold both flaps in half by folding them backward.

10. Fold the left point down toward the back.

11. Add eyes if desired.

Sperm Whale

Palaoa

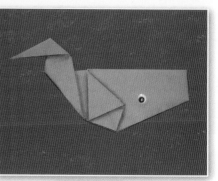

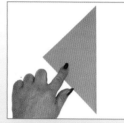

1. Fold the paper in half diagonally.

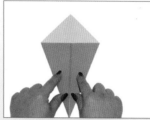

2. Open the fold. Fold the bottom edges inward to the center crease.

3. Open the folds. Fold the top edges inward to the center crease.

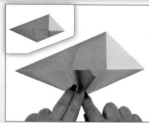

4. Turn the model. Open the bottom fold. Fold the bottom edges of the paper up to the center crease. Line up the edges, creating a squared flap in the center. Pinch and press down the flap toward the right.

5. Turn the model. Repeat step #4 by opening the bottom fold. Fold the bottom edges of the paper up to the center crease. Line up the edges, creating a squared flap in the center. Pinch and press down the flap toward the left.

6. Flip the model. Position the flaps on the bottom facing the left. Fold the right point inward.

7. Fold the model in half, positioning the flaps on the outside. Fold from top to bottom.

8. Turn the model. Push the flaps forward on both sides of the model. Bend down and tuck in the tips of the flaps.

9. Fold both flaps backward at an angle.

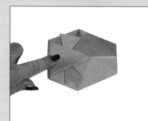

10. Open the center fold. Fold in the left point just past the flaps.

11. Close the centerfold, positioning the flaps on the outside. Pull up the top point. Pinch to crease.

12. Open the top point. Fold the tip backward. Close the point. Pull out the tip of the point. Pinch to crease.

13. Add eyes if desired.